NEW ENGLAND
REFLECTIONS
1882 - 1907

WALTER HOWES   ALVAH HOWES   GEORGE HOWES

NEW ENGLAND REFLECTIONS

1882 - 1907

PHOTOGRAPHS BY THE HOWES BROTHERS

EDITED BY ALAN B. NEWMAN

FROM THE COLLECTION OF THE ASHFIELD HISTORICAL SOCIETY

FOREWORD BY RICHARD WILBUR   INTRODUCTION BY GERALD McFARLAND

PANTHEON BOOKS, NEW YORK

The captions for the photographs reproduced here were written
expressly for the publication of this book.

Library of Congress Cataloging in Publication Data
Main entry under title:
New England reflections.
1. Photography, Artistic. 2. Connecticut
Valley—Description and travel—Views. 3. Howes,
Alvah. 4. Howes, George. 5. Howes, Walter.
I. Howes, Alvah. II. Howes, George. III. Howes,
Walter. IV. Newman, Alan B. V. Ashfield Historical Society.
TR652.N47   779'.997442041   80—8656
ISBN 0—394—51375—4
0—394—74912—x pbk.

Duotone negatives prepared by Doug Mitchell, Graphic Specialties,
Brooklyn, New York. Composed by Maryland Linotype Composition
Co., Inc., Baltimore, Maryland. Printed by Rae Publishing Co., Inc.,
Cedar Grove, New Jersey. Bound by American Book-Stratford Press,
Saddle Brook, New Jersey. Production directed by Peter Mollman and
Patrick Lee. Designed by Susan Mitchell.

To Kimball Howes and Theodore Hendrick,
who made it possible

ACKNOWLEDGMENTS

This book is a child of the Howes Brothers Photographic Preservation Project. The project represented a unique cooperative effort between the active membership of a small-town historical society, art and heritage agencies of the federal and state governments, photographic conservators and museum people, a publisher, historians, archivists, bibliographers, private foundations, and a large grassroots group of private contributors. We would like to take this opportunity to express our appreciation to the hundreds who have given their time and talents, and to thank in particular the following persons.

The Board of Trustees of the Ashfield Historical Society and the Committee on the Howes Photographic Project: Douglas Angleman, initial chairman of the committee and authorizing official of the NHPRC grant, a meticulous record keeper and financial analyst; Clayton Craft, president of the Ashfield Historical Society and early member of the committee; Norma Harris, AHS curator, who has spent more than fifteen years accumulating information about the Howes photographs and is the chief cataloguer for the Howes project; Theodore Hendrick, who has spent more than a dozen years researching the sites in the photographs and, through remarkable detective work, has made an invaluable contribution to the Howes catalogue; Kimball Howes, grandson of Walter, who made biographical and vintage photographic material available and gave support to this book and the project; John Kendall, Anglo-American studies bibliographer of the University of Massachusetts library, who offered essential assistance in the funding, planning, and conceptual framework of the Howes project; Carrolle Markle, who spearheaded the "impossible" task of matching a large federal grant, showing limitless energy and skill; Harriet Pike, former president of the AHS, who gave considerable time to help bring the right people together; and Norman Pike, who first encouraged the society to seek outside funding to help save the collection.

Dee Edwards worked admirably as a darkroom and catalogue assistant and made my work easier than it might have been. Among the consultants, Eugene Ostroff, chief curator of photography at the Smithsonian Institution, served as technical adviser; Andrew Eskind, director of curatorial services of the International Museum of Photography at George Eastman House, was the principal bibliographic expert, helping to design a descriptive/retrieval system assisted by computer for the information in the Howes photographs; Mike Kennedy, chief of the photolab at Harvard College Observatory, made all of the important sensitometric tests which helped us innovate a system for copying the negatives onto fine-grain motion-picture stock; Dan Jones and Chris Burnett, photoarchivists for Harvard's Peabody Museum, did important parallel research in copying techniques (it was Dan who first suggested using motion-picture film); and Lee Nadel helped me initially in printing the photographs after the first Howes grant.

Mr. and Mrs. Raymond Reniff and Mr. and Mrs. Lawrence VanCor made the first donations of many thousands of Howes negatives to the Ashfield Historical Society Museum. Florence Scott, the daughter of Ethel Bates, a Howes assistant, donated many vintage prints. Most of the historical societies that received Howes negatives in the 1960s have generously de-accessioned, or permanently loaned, their holdings to the Ashfield Historical Society Museum. Many individuals within these organizations helped with cataloguing information: the Cummington Historical Commission, in particular William Streeter and Olive Thayer, who first showed me Howes work in 1976; the Montague Historical Society and Marion Lombard; the Charlemont Historical Society and Ivis Russell; the Amherst Historical Society and Virginia Johnson; and historical societies in the towns of Millers Falls, Historic Deerfield, Easthampton, Southampton, Williamsburg, Northfield, Buckland, and Whately, Massachusetts.

The funding for the project came as a matching grant from the National Historical Publications and Records Commission; Larry Hackman and Nancy Sahli of NHPRC provided valuable guidance. Other important funding sources were the Massachusetts Council of the Arts and Humanities, with Nancy Padnos giving counsel; the (Lawrence) Miller Foundation; Mrs. Edwin Land; the Polaroid Foundation; the DeWitt Wallace (Reader's Digest) Foundation; Greenfield Community College, with Peg Howland facilitating; and Pantheon Books. John Szarkowski, head of the photography department of the Museum of Modern Art, helped considerably with his endorsement of the project; and Judson Rees, of Ashfield, gave counsel in grant writing.

George Rosa, president of the Hallmark Institute of Photography, Turners Falls, Massachusetts, donated the photographic paper.

David Stemple, of the University of Massachusetts Computer Center, designed the computer catalogue program. Paul Norton, professor of architectural history at the University of Massachusetts, conceived an authority list of architectural terms. Valuable time was volunteered in negative cleaning, indexing, and transferral to archival storage. Thomas Burnham, an AHS member, Dee Edwards, a CETA employee, and David Cote and Ronald Bennett, CETA high school students, helped in this regard, as did the following students in the Hampshire Educational Collaborative Media Project: Tad Mosher, Michael Rice, Darlene Trumble, Fran Twarog, Denise Laroche, and Jim Chartier.

Weston J. Naef, associate curator, Department of Prints and Photographs at the Metropolitan Museum of Art, contributed valuable suggestions for the editing of photographs in the first Howes platinum portfolio. Richard Benson, Sal Lopes, Mike Kennedy, and especially Lois Conner have shared with me over the years technical information in the craft of platinum printing.

The editing of the photographs for this book was a two-stage process. In the first stage, Dee Edwards, Gerald McFarland, Ted Hendrick, Norma Harris, and I selected a rough cut of 1,000 photographs. The final selections and sequences were principally a collaboration between Wendy Wolf of Pantheon and me. Ms. Wolf helped considerably with my manuscript, giving it form and coherence, and I was also influenced by the research of Professor McFarland. Fabio Coen of Knopf and Ashfield got the book off the ground, acting as the initial conduit between the Berkshires and New York. I appreciate the time Richard Wilbur devoted to writing his foreword, which is a well-honed reflection on these remarkable photographers.

Lastly, I must thank my wife, Katie, who endured these past several years with images of the past floating throughout our home, and gave support and encouragement to all phases of the book and the project.

ALAN B. NEWMAN
Ashfield, Massachusetts
December 1980

FOREWORD

If you live in this part of New England, the pictures taken by the Howes brothers of Ashfield can give you a momentarily jumbled sense of time. That is because so much of western Massachusetts and its periphery has proved unimprovable, and looks something as it did eighty or ninety years ago. There is never any doubt, to be sure, that in turning these pages one is looking into the past; it is a horse-drawn, unpaved, and largely un-mechanized world that one sees, and the decor and cloth-ing are a dead giveaway. Still, if you turn off the big highways anywhere in Howes territory and let the roads rise, twist, and narrow amidst trees and stone walls, you will soon see the generic house which the brothers so frequently recorded. It is a rather stark clapboard house, perhaps with a narrow front porch and a shed and barn adjoining. You would not say that the grounds had been landscaped, though the old rock maples are beautiful; there may be a bit of litter about—a board, a barrow, an overturned tub which seems to have been there a while. A grape arbor, very likely; a garden, an orchard, stony fields. Behind all, you will see for certain the wooded hills as they always were, their dark conifer patches striated with birch, and above them a sky which knows how to be cold in season. Some social scientist tells us that 85 percent of Americans now live in city or suburb, in much-changed or developed communities where the awareness of topog-raphy is dimmed. What would a Dallasite recognize in a picture of old Dallas? But certain pictures in the Howes archive convey to me an odd first impression of familiar vistas infiltrated by strangers.

One reason why Howes photography can affect you so is that it has none of the haze and chiaroscuro of memory, of history; though pointedly composed, the pictures take in everything on equal terms, and the least detail comes forward sharply. That tangle of elderberry, fox-grape, and wild cherry is just down our road on the right-hand side, this minute; that sledge hammer standing on its head by a wall is the image of mine. Another reason for the partial illusion of presentness is that the people, with their period air and attire, are so often subordinated to representations of structures and farmsteads, of interiors, of enterprises, of groups and of group labor. I am told that the Howes brothers' advance-man, going from town to town, secured commissions for the recording of family, commercial, or institutional history; when the photog-rapher came, it was not to do impressions of the landscape or portraits of isolate heads, but to record milieus, gather-ings, whole aspects of the world's work. These photo-graphs are of a special sort, then—documentary in inten-tion, answering the customer's desire, displaying people in the midst of their settings and undertakings. Old family albums of the time, or the products of portrait studios, would give us other glimpses of the same world; but these, I think, have something more or different to tell.

In good light, the Howes camera could take a fifth-of-a-second exposure, so that the catatonic expressions of an earlier day were not necessary. Nevertheless, it is fairly seldom that these faces, which look as a rule toward the camera, are smiling or projecting personality. Eight bundled-up men and women, about to push off for a bob-sled ride, are full of gaiety and expectation; seated on his front stoop with his shoes on a city sidewalk, a solid man with a well-fed family, a derby, bow tie, and watch chain, lets us know that he is an aggressive man of business; two stylish adolescent boys with knotted scarves are the only subjects, in the pictures I happen to have sampled, who regard the lens with a sleek and amused complacency. On the lawn behind them is a hammock emblematic of leisure. Most convey little of polish or well-to-do ease. A wedding party in a pasture is uniformly grave, though the bride's ducked head may be hiding a shy smile; the grandmother giving an infant its bottle is frowningly blank; dwarfed by a barnlike house at the corner of Pine Street, a family stares at us with expressionless faces. Is it diffidence we see in such cases? Stoicism? A lingering Calvinist austerity? Possibly, but I think also of what one of the Adamses said—that the pitiful thing is not to be poor, but to feel that one does not matter. Surely, to face a camera, especially a professional one, was not an everyday thing for some of these folk. I suspect that their seriousness of mien has often to do with a sense that their lives for once are going on record, that however modestly, they are entering history.

Am I permitted one more catalogue? In these studies not of single selves but of interrelated lives and their properties, there is a wish to *show* as much as possible; the whole family and its homestead, with the horse and wagon on display; the grade-school class putting forward the potted plants they have tended; the man who, torn between exhibiting his work and its fruits, wears a Sunday suit and hat while holding a calf on a halter; the busy barbershop seen *in toto*, from the front door clear to the shelved bottles in the back; the tobacco workers showing the process of rolling the cheesecloth after the harvest; the timber gang showing you how they work together. Workers, in these pictures, are generally more at ease than those who have nothing to do but pose, but the salient thing about them is not personality but function: this is a man, you say, who is proud of his axe-work; there is a fellow who can use a peavey. Perhaps the height of personal effacement is the photo of a man who has somehow managed to get a yardful of leashed dogs to hold still; the one thing blurred is his face.

Some of the descendants of the Howes brothers' subjects have doubtless enjoyed this century's mobility, its pursuit of self-fulfillment, its softer and glossier ways of living. Having had their pictures taken amidst the pigeons of the Piazza di San Marco, they may look with little yearning on the pages of this book. Still, what we mostly see here is a self-respecting breed who knew how to do many things, who knew who they were, who made themselves comfortable enough, who had their recreations, were more cohesive than we, and were closer than we to a sometimes hard but always beautiful land. It is not a bad picture.

RICHARD WILBUR
Cummington, Massachusetts

The Howes brothers,—Alvah, Walter, and George— were natives of Ashfield, a village in the Berkshire hills of western Massachusetts. Their father, George Howes, had a small farm and a large family (five sons and two daughters), which may explain why four of his sons decided to leave home in search of a better livelihood. Of the four, William found employment as a factory hand, while Alvah, Walter, and George eventually entered the field of commercial photography, a profession that expanded rapidly after the Civil War. During their active

years as professional photographers (1886–1906), the three brothers worked largely as itinerants, traveling from place to place and taking pictures of households, school classes, factory crews, shopkeepers, delivery men, and virtually anyone or anything else they could get to stand still long enough. More than 20,000 glass-plate negatives taken by the Howes brothers survive. Valuable as social documents, rich in visual information about New England people and scenes, these photographs are also eloquent testimony to the industry and artistry of the Howes brothers themselves.

Any history of the Howes brothers must begin with Alvah, the eldest of George Howes's sons and the one who first took up photography. Born in 1853, Alvah grew up on his father's Ashfield farm and attended the neighborhood common school. Nothing else is known of his youth to distinguish it from that of other hill-town farm boys of the period. As late as 1880, when Alvah was twenty-six, he was still living in Ashfield, working as a farm laborer for Henry Ranney, an older neighbor and friend.

Precisely when and how Alvah became a photographer remains a puzzle. Fragmentary evidence suggests he entered the profession in the mid-1880s, perhaps through a connection with a man named Elliott W. Cook, who lived in the Ranney homestead where Alvah boarded. In the 1880 census, Cook listed his occupation as "traveling agent," but later in the decade he practiced photography, giving an Albany, New York address on his prints. Whether Alvah received his early training from Cook or worked with him is not known, but there was clearly some link between the two men's careers since several photographs taken in the mid-1880s have Cook backings with Cook's name crossed out and *A. W. Howes* printed in its place. The earliest verifiable dates for Alvah's photographic career are 1886 and 1887, when he and his brother Walter toured as itinerants. In 1888 Alvah opened a studio in Turners Falls, Massachusetts, calling his firm A. W. Howes & Company and employing a variety of assistants, including Walter (and occasionally the youngest Howes brother, George), to help with work outside Turners Falls.

All the Howes photographs were made on glass dry-plate negatives, an improved technology that became widely available in the late 1870s. Factory-coated dry-plate negatives had numerous advantages over the older daguerreotype and collodion methods, particularly for small-time, traveling photographers. The daguerreotype method, which yielded only a single copy, was unsuitable for photographers like the Howes brothers who depended heavily on sales of multiple copies, often to large groups—school classes, factory crews, and family reunions. The collodion or wet-plate method produced a negative from which prints could be made, but it was a cumbersome process that required considerable technical skill and a large investment in equipment. (See Afterword for more on these techniques.) The transformation of the Howes brothers from farmers into photographers, therefore, was facilitated by the development of easy-to-handle, low-cost dry-plate glass negatives.

Particularly in its early years, the Howes firm was a shoestring operation which succeeded, in part, because the brothers received help from family and friends. In 1886, for example, when Alvah and Walter began touring in the "view business," as Walter called it, they went first to Florence, Massachusetts, a town where they had family connections. During the winter months when the brothers were not touring, they holed up at the Howes homestead in Ashfield. The next spring, 1887, they moved their operation to South Coventry, Connecticut, and boarded with their brother William, who was employed there as a hand in his father-in-law's box factory. While in South Coventry, Walter fell in love with Ida Wolfram, a German-born woman who worked in a local mill. Later that summer, while the brothers stayed at Mrs. Dean's boardinghouse in nearby South Manchester, a romance began between Alvah and the landlady's daughter Eliza. The brothers married their respective sweethearts in 1888.

Walter's letters to his fiancée during 1888 provide invaluable information about the Howes brothers' organization and working methods. As the firm's senior member, Alvah took responsibility for managing the studio in Turners Falls, providing a home base where photographs taken by the itinerants were printed. The touring part of the company generally involved a team of three men. Walter and a neighbor from Ashfield, Harry Sturtevant,

took turns taking the photographs, while the third member, either young George Howes or "a Ranney boy" from Ashfield, drove the photographers' wagon and ran various errands. Upon their arrival in a town that they planned to work, the trio would first arrange for bed and board at a local rooming house. They would then set about soliciting customers, visiting schools and factories to line up orders for group sessions and driving along town streets and country roads, knocking on doors to invite people to have their pictures taken. Prints were sold at three for a dollar.

The itinerant threesome seldom stayed in a single location more than six weeks. June 1888 found them boarding with Sturtevant's mother in Greenfield. In a typical letter to Ida, Walter reported that he and George had been working a road outside Millers Falls, a town roughly ten miles from Greenfield. Over a two-day period they took forty-eight pictures. They planned to move to Pittsfield, Massachusetts, in July, but on hearing that the Pittsfield area "had been worked some" they went instead to Shelburne Falls, where the cutlery plant was about to reopen and where the Howes brothers had an aunt and uncle. In mid-August they relocated in Bennington, Vermont, and quickly drummed up business with several fire companies, the local hosiery mills, and a school district that had more than five hundred pupils. An unexpected bonus came when one man they had photographed was shot to death while they were still in town. Prints of him, Walter dryly noted to Ida, "are selling verry [sic] well[;] it is a poor wind that blows no one any good." Early in October they decided to divide forces for a time. Sturtevant and Ranney moved on to begin work in Hoosick Falls, New York, while Walter remained in Bennington to deliver prints.

Although Walter apparently enjoyed his life as a touring "photo man," he occasionally complained about the less attractive side of the work. Among the occupational hazards he mentioned most frequently were bad weather, constant changes in diet, and cramped quarters in boardinghouses—one bedroom which the three men occupied, Walter claimed, measured no more than eight feet by nine.

Yet in spite of these discomforts, one, two, and often all three Howes brothers chose to lead this life of seasonal movement—winters in Ashfield followed by semi-gypsy status from April to November—every year from 1886 to 1902.

Between 1888 and 1894, Alvah did not share this peripatetic existence but occupied himself with the management of his photographic gallery in Turners Falls. For the first five of those years, at least, he enjoyed considerable business success, building his clientele through clever promotions. In 1889, for instance, he offered a "photograph of itself free to every baby less than 18 months old" that came to his studio on certain days. Two weeks later the local newspaper, the *Turners Falls Reporter*, announced that 105 babies had taken advantage of the offer. Christmas specials offering fifteen "cabinet photographs" (4-by-6-inch prints) for the price of a dozen and bean-guessing contests with a free portrait as the prize were featured in his advertising campaigns. One series of advertisements began with the headline "HAVE MAMA'S PICTURE TAKEN." The advertisement was repeated for months thereafter, but with a different relative mentioned each week—"Little Sister," "Grandma," "Papa," "Baby," and so on—until every imaginable relative had been mentioned. At that point patrons were urged to have "Kittie's" and "The Dog's" portraits taken.

In October 1894, the forward progress of Alvah's photography career came to a crashing halt. With debts of nearly $1,300 and assets of less than $500, Alvah felt compelled to declare insolvency: a victim of the national depression that began in 1893. As the *Turners Falls Reporter* put it, "The village was dumbfounded, last week, when the report got out that A. W. Howes, the photographer, had failed." Dependent on doing a large-volume business, he simply could not maintain sufficient cash flow as money grew tighter and many of his prospective customers decided photographs were something they could forgo. Alvah's creditors, among them several Howes relatives, soon agreed to a settlement of twenty-five cents on the

dollar. Alvah left Turners Falls and returned to Ashfield in January 1895.

Alvah bounced back quickly. Turning to his brother George for financial backing, he reorganized his company, naming it A. W. & G. E. Howes. The three Howes brothers went on the road together in 1896, and again each spring for the next six years. Faithful practitioners of their trade, they photographed their entourage in front of the houses they occupied while touring (as seen on page 129). At least one member of the troupe, the person who snapped the picture (usually Alvah), was missing from the photograph. The fullest portrait of the Howes road company, therefore, is a statistical one in the 1900 census. The census taker found the itinerants early in June at Florence, Massachusetts. Alvah and his wife were renting a house on North Maple, and Ethel Rice, one of Alvah's assistants, was boarding with them. On Chestnut Street, barely three blocks away, Walter and George had rented a house suitable for ten occupants—the two brothers, their wives (George having married in 1898), Walter and Ida's three children, and two assistant photographers, one of whom was accompanied by his wife.

Although the Howes entourage was much larger in 1900 than in 1890 or 1886, the brothers continued to travel far afield in search of business. Most years, they changed addresses two or three times. Operating in this fashion, the brothers covered quite a bit of New England geography between 1886, when they first kept records, and 1902, their last year together on the road. Forays into eastern New England in the 1890s took them, among other places, to Woonsocket, Rhode Island, Waltham, Massachusetts, and Manchester, New Hampshire. Occasionally they crossed into sections of New York State and Vermont along the Massachusetts border. However, it was in two areas closer to their home in Ashfield—the Berkshire hills of western Massachusetts and the Connecticut River valley from the Massachusetts-Vermont border south to Hartford, Connecticut—that the brothers spent the most time and took the most photographs.

The world one glimpses through the Howes photographs is a land of contrasts. The difference between Lowell, an important industrial city of roughly 90,000 when the Howeses summered there in 1899, and Hawley, a tiny Berkshire village (population 545 in 1895), probably needs little elaboration. However, even in the Connecticut River valley and Berkshire hill regions one encounters a varied physical landscape. With the exception of Pittsfield and North Adams, the prevailing environment in the Berkshires was (and is) the rural town, the small village whose spirit Richard Wilbur evokes so gracefully in his foreword to this volume. Ashfield, Buckland, Chesterfield, Cummington, Hinsdale, Huntington, Lanesboro, Plainfield, Shelburne Falls, Worthington, to name but a few: most of these villages had less than 1,000 inhabitants in 1900. By contrast the Connecticut River valley, though there were also many villages in the region, was dominated by larger towns and cities. Among these, the town of Greenfield near the Vermont border was relatively small (population 6,229 in 1895), but in the mid-1880s a traveler headed southward through the valley soon reached more populous places—Northampton (16,746), Holyoke (40,322), Chicopee (16,420), and Springfield (51,522).

In the late nineteenth century the fortunes of the Berkshires and the Connecticut River valley were on distinctly different trajectories. During the twenty years that Alvah Howes was active as a photographer, the population of most hill towns either remained stable or declined slightly. This pattern, which dated back to the 1860s or before, contrasted dramatically with the swift expansion taking place in the Connecticut River valley. In the decade between 1895 and 1905 alone Greenfield's population grew by nearly 47 percent, Springfield's by almost 43 percent, Holyoke's by approximately 24 percent, and Northampton's by slightly more than 19 percent.

The Howes brothers' photographs offer mute testimony to these diverging patterns. Little new construction is evident in the pictures of hill-town scenes, and some of the most poignant subjects are elderly country people, their bent frames echoing the sagging rooflines of their homes. Both house and householder had seen better days. In the valley, on the other hand, the population boom led to widespread new construction, and the Howes photographs of valley locales include numerous pictures of houses and streets with a newly landscaped, just-completed look about them.

The Connecticut valley boom towns and the Berkshire villages represented two different Americas, the one emerging, the other passing. Yet the distinctions between the two regions should not be oversimplified. Though the Berkshires were largely rural, the region's economy was by no means exclusively agricultural. On the contrary, the Howes camera recorded abundant examples of hill-town industrial establishments, dating from the mid-nineteenth century. In Cummington the brothers photographed the crew of the local paper mill. In Shelburne Falls many of their customers were employees of the town's cutlery plant. Tiny Richmond had an ironworks, Haydenville a brass factory, Huntington a woolens mill, and West Stockbridge several marble and lime quarries. Thus, in addition to the sawmills and maple-sugar houses that survive even now in the region, a host of other small industries were found throughout the Berkshires. Farm-implement factories, textile mills, brickyards, gristmills, and box factories, most of them employing no more than twenty-five workers, dotted the hill towns.

The hill-town mills serve as reminders that much of America's early industrial revolution took place in small-scale production units located outside urban centers. Many Berkshire villages had enjoyed an industrial boom prior to the Civil War largely because the primary power source in the period was water, and the villages had plenty of that. Industrial growth enabled some villages which had been losing their sons and daughters to richer Western farmlands early in the 1800s to regain population in the 1830s and 1840s. After the Civil War, however, increased industrial concentration and new power sources—first steam, then electricity—prompted construction of huge

factories along the Connecticut River which required much larger work forces than the Berkshire villages could provide. Gradually, the hill-town mills lost out competitively.

The history of industry in Cummington, Massachusetts, mirrors these trends in microcosm. In its heyday prior to the Civil War, Cummington had four tanneries, three gristmills, ten sawmills, four woolen goods mills, a large cotton factory, and ten mills of other types. The town reached its peak population, 1,237, in the same period. Toward the end of the century, when the Howes brothers photographed the Cummington paper factory, only a few other local mills remained in operation, and the town's population was down one-third from its peak. Even the paper mill's days were numbered. Built in 1856, having employed as many as twenty-five hands, and having been the first local mill to hire women, it closed its doors for keeps in August 1908.

Villages like Cummington exemplified a social and economic milieu that Robert Wiebe has labeled the "island community." Even as industrialization was creating a more nationalized society—one in which most communities depended increasingly on sources outside themselves for food, manufactured goods, and even entertainment— the island communities for a time remained relatively self-sufficient. Images of this older way of life abound in the

Howes photographs of Berkshire mills, villages, people, and schools. Water, a local resource, drove the machinery in village factories. People generally traveled in buggies and wagons built by local carriage makers and drawn by horses fed with hay and grain raised on local farms. Repairs were made by blacksmiths, their small shops as essential to the island community's well-being as gasoline stations are to modern suburban life. Sawmills along the towns' rivers, stone quarries, and local brickworks supplied the materials for house construction. Such basic needs as water and sanitation were met through wells and outhouses. Education took place in the one-room school, an institution which epitomized local control. Class sizes, to judge from hundreds of Howes school pictures, were small. There were usually between ten and fifteen students per class, as compared with classes of thirty-five to forty students commonplace in city school districts.

By the late nineteenth century the relative autonomy of the island communities was breaking down. Telephone lines and electric trolleys were two agencies of this transformation. The larger Connecticut valley towns were linked by telephone in the late 1880s. By the 1890s Bell system linemen were beginning to string telephone lines into the countryside. Village phone service at first was usually limited to a very few individual phones, a number of business subscribers, and a public phone at the town's

general store for everyone else's use. Restricted though the early service was, it tied the old island communities into an expanded communications network, thus greatly reducing the villages' physical isolation.

In the mid-1880s, electric trolleys appeared on the scene. Railroads, of course, had connected major towns and cities decades before this, and though they were highly efficient as carriers of passengers and freight between distant points, they were generally too expensive for frequent use by short-haul patrons such as commuters. Because electric trolley systems were cheaper to build and operate, they were readily adapted to meet commuter needs. The immediate effect was to open out cities, allowing residents to escape crowded inner-city areas for the so-called streetcar suburbs. The social consequences were enormous. Larger valley communities rapidly divided into inner-city and suburban districts, a pattern that prevails to the present. For commuters the place of work and place of residence became widely separated, a condition that tended to reinforce middle-class sex roles: the woman as a housewife, the man as a provider who dealt with the harsh realities of professional life. Also, for middle-class people who rushed to the streetcar suburbs, the move brought tangible material gains, notably the acquisition of larger homes with more spacious lots.

Trolley fever reached epidemic proportions between the mid-1880s and 1905. In city after city—for example, Holyoke in 1884 and Northampton in 1893—companies organized to build electric trolley systems. Not content with serving their own community and its suburbs, the trolley companies soon pushed lines outward toward neighboring cities and towns. Holyoke and Springfield were linked by an interurban line in 1895, the six-mile ride costing customers a dime. Over the next ten years an incredible network of trolley tracks spread through the Connecticut River valley. If one had enough time and transfers, it was possible to ride interurbans from Hartford, Connecticut, north to Greenfield, Massachusetts, near the Vermont border. Eventually the trolley mania spread from

the valley cities into the foothills of the Berkshires. A twenty-mile line from Springfield to Huntington, a hill town with less than fifteen hundred inhabitants, was completed in 1905. In the same period even more distant Berkshire villages like Cummington were angling, unsuccessfully as it turned out, for trolley service.

Perhaps the most imposing monuments to the new industrial society were the huge factories built in the larger Connecticut valley towns after the Civil War: massive brick structures four, five, or more stories tall, some of them covering a full city block. The Howes brothers often took pictures of such factories on speculation, hoping to sell copies to the mills' employees. It was a market well worth pursuing. Whereas factory work forces in hill towns typically numbered no more than two dozen employees, many valley mills employed two hundred or more workers and a few occasionally had more than a thousand employees. Products varied. Many of Holyoke's biggest mills were paper factories, but the city was also the home of Farr Alpaca, one of the largest worsted mills in the world. Holyoke's largest factory, however, was the Lyman Mills, a cotton textile concern whose buildings stretched for an eighth of a mile through the city's heart. During the bicycle craze of the 1880s and 1890s, the Overman Wheel Company in nearby Chicopee employed as many as twelve hundred workers and even so was hard pressed to meet the demand. Machine tools, firearms, cutlery, and shoes were but a few of the other items manufactured on a large scale in Holyoke, Chicopee, and elsewhere in the Connecticut River valley.

Broadly speaking, telephone lines, electric trolleys, and huge factories were manifestations of a social and economic revolution under way during the Howes brothers' active years as photographers. Harbingers of this new America appear frequently in the Howes photographs—a delivery truck for Rockefeller's Standard Oil Company, advertisements for Pillsbury's Flour, an occasional early automobile, and Bell Telephone signs. Yet it would be a mistake to assume that the world of the Howes brothers

underwent a complete transformation between 1886 and 1906. As late as 1900, a medium-sized town (c. 5,000) like Amherst, Massachusetts, could still boast an impressive array of small-scale local industries. Boxes, bricks, brooms, building materials, carriages and wagons, cigars, flour, hats, leather goods, lumber, and pumps were milled or manufactured in the town's small industrial establishments. The triumph of an emerging large-scale, corporate, national, and urban society over an older, more localized America was far from complete at the turn of the century.

Throughout this essay I have referred to the Howes photographs as documenting social and economic conditions in western New England during the late nineteenth century. It is important to recognize, however, that the Howes pictures were not taken for the purpose of creating a social history archive. The Howes brothers were entrepreneurs in business to sell pictures. Inevitably, this made them approach their trade differently from a famous New York contemporary, Jacob Riis. In taking photographs of slum people for his book *How the Other Half Lives*, Riis did not have to consider, as the Howes brothers always did, whether the results would please the people pictured. Riis was a social reformer whose selection of photographic subjects was shaped by the search for visual evidence in support of his reform ideas. By contrast, the Howes brothers selected subjects they hoped would result in

marketable pictures. Nevertheless, the Howeses' need to sell pictures also served, albeit inadvertently, the needs of future social historians.

The Howes brothers often made door-to-door canvasses for prospective customers. The typical result was a picture of people lined up in front of a house, a format that appears thousands of times in Howes prints and that provides a wealth of information about the people and places portrayed. Socially, the subjects ranged from well-to-do householders and their handsome homes to working-class people in front of their cramped shacks or tenements. Among both the poor and the prosperous, some individuals dressed up for the occasion. Others seem to have come direct from the kitchen or barn in their dirty aprons or tattered work clothes. Over all, the pictures provide an informal catalogue of clothing worn between 1886 and 1906, including the contrasting styles worn in town and country, by the middle class and working class, and by different generations (mothers and daughters, for instance).

The Howes firm's emphasis on a low-cost product also had beneficial side-effects for social historians. Among the working-class people in the Howes pictures were many individuals who might well have felt that a formal sitting at a photographic gallery in town was beyond their means. Even had they made a studio appointment, they doubtless would have treated it as a special occasion and worn their Sunday best. The Howes brothers knocked on their doors and promised an inexpensive print, making the whole process more accessible and spontaneous. Ordinary people often appear in their ordinary clothes and in front of their homes, some of which are shockingly small and shabby.

The Howes brothers displayed considerable versatility, pursuing their trade with apparent ease in both farm and urban areas and in working-class districts and middle-class neighborhoods. To some degree this may have been a matter of commercial necessity, of going where the market was, although an affinity for farmers and country scenes doubtless came naturally enough to the brothers, raised as they were on a farm. They also had many direct contacts with factory and industrial settings. George, the youngest, had done millwork for a time. William, a brother who did not take up photography, was for many years a factory hand. Alvah and Walter married women who had held manual jobs and whose relatives included ordinary laborers. The brothers completed grammar school, but went no further—sufficient schooling to make them comfortable with most middle-class people of the day, but not so much as to deprive them of the common touch in dealing with laborers and working-class families.

Although the Howes brothers were churchgoing, non-drinking Yankee Protestants, these traits and convictions seem not to have cut them off from any significant group of potential clients. In Massachusetts, for instance, Negroes composed only about 1 percent of the state's population, yet many blacks appear in the Howes photographs. More-over, black people turn up in a wide variety of roles, from very poor farmers and workers to well-dressed profes-sional and business people, including a woman school-teacher, a policeman, and two portraits of black women standing in front of their small business establishments.

The Howeses also numbered among their customers other non-Yankee ethnic groups—the Irish, French Cana-dian, Italian, and Slavic peoples who had recently migrated to western Massachusetts. Every Berkshire hill town had at least a few foreign-born residents, and in Ashfield alone

during the 1880s the brothers might have met people born in Ireland, Germany, Sweden, Switzerland, Canada, and England. In the Connecticut River valley, the brothers worked in cities with some of the highest concentrations of recent immigrants in the United States. In 1890 close to half of Holyoke's population was foreign-born, a higher percentage than any other American city except Fall River, Massachusetts, and Duluth, Minnesota. The faces of these new Americans appear with some regularity in Howes pictures of factory work crews and poorer urban neighbor-hoods. Howes photographs of Catholic parochial schools with classes posed under the watchful eye of a nun in her black habit serve as reminders that the newcomers were mostly non-Protestants.

The Howes brothers habitually urged clients to bring objects they particularly valued to the photographic ses-sion. Workers often carried the tools of their trade, and families lined up with their prize possessions—everything from oxen, chickens, and pets (innumerable dogs and cats and at least one bowl of fish) to lawn mowers, farm equipment, and the household's best chair. Horses of all varieties appear in great numbers—high-spirited buggy horses, heavy draft horses, light farm horses, and riding horses. Hints of the era's recreational habits are conveyed by pictures of boys with bats and mitts, children with hoops and dolls, numerous bicycles, and an occasional rowboat. Hammocks and porch swings recall the summer pastimes of a pre-television age. Lastly, though not in the category of favored possessions, there are the character-istic poses of the day, notably the hands-on-hips posture that many subjects adopted when facing the camera.

Among all these images, every viewer will doubtless find a few surprises. People unfamiliar with the Con-necticut River valley may be startled to find that leaf tobacco for wrapping cigars was (and is) a prime cash crop in the region. The tiny shacks and run-down farm-houses in some Howes photographs are a far cry from the spacious homes with mansard roofs and elaborate exterior decoration popularly associated with Victorian architecture. Nor do the weary farm folk and the shabbily dressed working-class families in the Howes pictures fit very well with the stereotypical description of the decade known as the Gay Nineties.

Women, too, are pictured in ways that belie the conventional image of late-nineteenth-century women as frail and overprotected stay-at-homes whose husbands, fathers, and brothers did all the hard work of the day. Numerous Howes prints show women actively taking supposedly masculine roles—holding the buggy's reins or leading farm animals out to be photographed. Office secretaries were clearly members of the salaried work force. Hundreds of Howes pictures of school classes confirm that female teaching staffs were the backbone of the American educational system. As for industrial labor, group portraits of factory crews show that a significant proportion of millworkers were women. Indeed, women constituted as much as 50 percent of the factory employees in Holyoke, one of the valley's most important industrial centers.

Although this catalogue of gleanings from the Howes photographs could be extended, no such listing can or should pretend to be exhaustive. In the end, what viewers see will depend largely on their own ingenuity and interests. A careful student of the whole Howes collection, however, might note a slight shrinkage in the range of subject matter in the photographs after 1902, largely be-

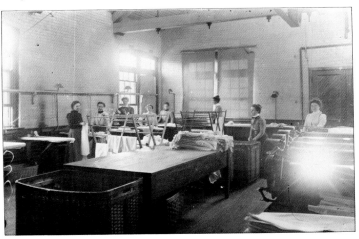

cause 1902 was the last year that Alvah, Walter, and George Howes toured together as itinerant photographers. Precisely why they decided to quit is not known. Perhaps the increasing popularity of flexible roll film and Kodak hand cameras (available since the mid-1890s) made their itinerant photography business less profitable. Perhaps, too, the brothers were simply growing weary of a career that kept them on the road so much of the year. In any case, when Walter and George had an opportunity to buy out a cousin's interest in a Northampton-Florence area trucking firm, they leaped at the chance. Alvah moved back to Ashfield for good in 1903 and continued his professional work, but even he, the first in the business and the last of the brothers to leave it, was soon to quit.

Changes in Alvah's personal life may account in part for his decision to abandon his career of twenty years' standing. His first wife, Eliza, died in 1904. They had no living children. (A son born in 1891 died the very same day, a personal tragedy that may have reinforced Alvah's penchant for photographing babies.) Alvah remarried in 1905. His second wife was Ida Chaffee, a Holyoke housekeeper whom he may have met through his first wife's family. After his remarriage Alvah became even less active as a photographer, limiting himself mainly to business in the Ashfield area. His last identifiable commercial photographs seem to have been taken in 1906 or 1907. About that time he returned to farming, running a small dairy farm in Ashfield. He also served the town as its lamplighter and helped maintain Ashfield's small cemeteries. He died on November 25, 1919.

Beginning in 1903, Walter and George Howes cooperated in a series of business ventures, an express and trucking firm, a brickyard, and finally lumber and construction projects. George died in 1925. Walter remained in Florence near many scenes he and his brothers had photographed years before. The memory of the family's photographic enterprises dimmed in time, but never disappeared completely, as an incident from the 1940s illustrates. One of Walter's grandsons became interested in photography and asked his father (Walter's son Wallace, who as a young boy had accompanied his father and uncles on tour) the whereabouts of the family's old photographic equipment. There was some discussion of where the old cameras might be, but somehow they never turned up. Walter, the grandfather and last surviving Howes brother, died in 1945.

Fortunately, the Howes brothers' story does not end there. In the mid-1960s two Ashfield couples, in separate gifts, each gave the Ashfield Historical Society thousands of Howes glass-plate negatives. Subsequently other public-spirited individuals donated additional negatives and prints, bringing the society's Howes collection to its present size of more than 20,000 items. In the mid-1970s the Ashfield Historical Society sponsored a successful drive to fund the preservation and microfilming of the Howes negatives,

and in 1980 the Howes Brothers Photographic Preservation Project was completed.

In recent years the work of the Howes brothers has attracted increasing attention, and rightly so. As an archive of photographs by a single family firm, the Howes collection is unusually large, perhaps the largest of its type in the United States. For students of photography, it will doubtless yield valuable insights into the art and practice of late-nineteenth-century itinerant photographers. For social historians, the collection is a significant source of information on the New England locales where the brothers practiced their trade between 1886 and 1906. By any standard, therefore—quantity and quality, importance historically and photographically—the Howes collection is a major one, a rich legacy of three diligent craftsmen: Alvah, Walter, and George Howes.

GERALD W. MCFARLAND
University of Massachusetts, Amherst

NEW ENGLAND REFLECTIONS 1882 - 1907

I   THE BEGINNING

2   STEADYING THE ROCKER

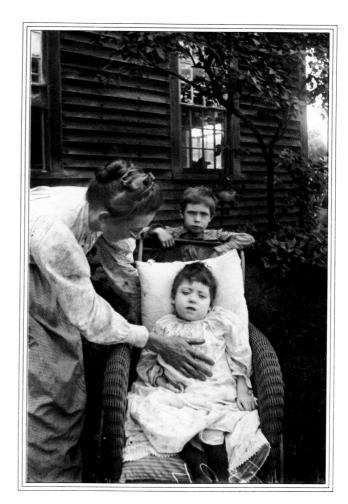

3   COMFORT TO THE CHILD

4   THREE GENERATIONS

5   INFANT AND ONLOOKERS

6   MOTHERING

7   MEDITERRANEAN FAMILY WITH SWADDLED TWINS

8   FAMILY AND SERVANTS

9   IVY LEAGUE PILLOWS

10   BLACK FAMILY WITH RELUCTANT ONLOOKER

II   THE GARDNER FAMILY

I2   A WELL-TO-DO BLACK FAMILY

13   BACKYARD GROUP

14   FAMILY

15   BICYCLES AND SUNDAY DRESSES

16   THE AUTUMN OF THEIR YEARS

17   BLACK MAN, BICYCLE,
AND HOWES BROTHERS' BUGGY

18   RABBI

19   POLICEMAN

20   VETERAN

21   MY CRUTCHES

22   APRON, GEOMETRY, AND LIGHT
(Worthington, Mass.)

23   HAT, HANDKERCHIEF, AND AN EMPTY CHAIR

24   BAREFOOT MUSICIAN AND BROTHER
(Feeding Hills, Mass.)

25   URBAN WORKING-CLASS SCENE
(Wilbraham, Mass.)

26   KIDDIE LOCOMOTION

27   FRANK HOWES (*Ashfield, Mass.*)

28   WHITE DRESS, WHITE PONY (*Suffield, Conn.*)

29   EQUINE PRIDE

30   ROCKING-HORSE TWINS

31   THIS IS WHAT THEY DO BEST

32   BRILLIANT ANGORA

33   CHICKEN FEEDING

34   TO FEED THE FAMILY

35 MESSRS. ROOT AND BITZER, WITH AN OXEN-LOAD
OF CORN FODDER (*Montague, Mass.*)

36 THE WARGER FAMILY (*Ashfield, Mass.*)

37   SILAGE LOADER POWERED BY STEAM TRACTOR
(Montague, Mass.)

38   RELUCTANT TOBACCO WORKER

39   STRETCHING THE NETS

40   UNDER THE TOBACCO NETS

41   DOG TRAINER (*Pelham, Mass.*)

42   H A R V E S T   (*North Westfield Street, Feeding Hills, Mass.*)

43   S O R T I N G   T O B A C C O

44   MEN AMONG THE TOBACCO LEAVES (*Little River Road, Westfield, Mass.*)

45   GREENHOUSE, EARLY SPRING

46   GREENHOUSE PALMS

47 ASA PHILLIPS AND
FRANK PRENTISS, COON HUNTERS

48 IN THE FIELD

49   ORCHARD WORKERS *(Cummington, Mass.?)*

50   CIDER MILL

51   BEEKEEPER (*Williamsburg, Mass.*)

52   BARN AND PRODUCE

53   PLOWING *(Montague, Mass.)*

54   OCTAGONAL BARN

55   BUTCHERING

56   BUTTER AND CHEESE IN THE DAIRY (*Easthampton, Mass.*)

57   LOGGERS I

58   LOGGERS II (*North Cemetery, Gill, Mass.*)

59   LOGGERS WITH PROUD AXE

60   S A W M I L L   (*West Springfield, Mass.*)

61   S T E A M - P O W E R E D   S A W M I L L

62   BARN RAISING

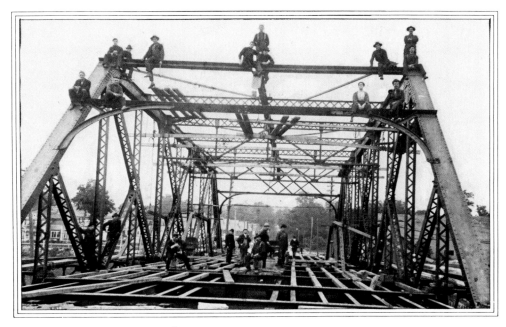

63   BRIDGE BUILDERS

64   B R I C K Y A R D I (*Amherst, Mass.*)

65   B R I C K Y A R D I I (*Amherst, Mass.*)

66   B R I C K W O R K S

67   BRICKMAKERS

68   STEAM DRILLING IN THE QUARRY

68A   THE FOUNDATION (*Buckland, Mass.*)

69   QUARRY WORKERS

70   MINE BUILDINGS

71   COOPERS WITH THEIR BARRELS

72   STONECUTTING

73   HOUSE PAINTERS

74   UP AND . . . (*Bernardston, Mass.?*)

75   . . . OVER (*Bernardston, Mass.?*)

76　　P L A N T　(*Bernardston, Mass.*)

77　　F O U N D R Y　(*E. Horton & Son, Chuck Castings*)

78   IN THE LAUNDRY

79   WORKERS' HOUSING (*Canal and Fifth Streets, Turners Falls, Mass.*)

80   MILL ON THE RIVER *(Bernardston, Mass.)*

81   GRADING THE ROAD

82   PREPARING TO LAY A ROAD

83   LINEMEN (*Cummington, Mass.*)

84   STEAMROLLER

85   AQUEDUCT INSTALLATION

86   BRIDGE ABUTMENT CREW (*Glendale Street, Easthampton, Mass.*)

87   TROLLEY (*Glastonbury Line, Conn.*)

88   LAYING TRACK

89   FLAGMAN (*Buckland, Mass.*)

TRAIN STATION INTERIOR

91   STEARNS & ARCHIBALD, PROPS. (*Northfield, Mass.*)

92   WARD BLOCK (*Millers Falls, Mass.*)

93   TOWN HALL AND CRAFTS STORE (*Ashfield, Mass.*)

94   M O N T A G U E T A V E R N *(Montague, Mass.)*

95   A S H F I E L D H O U S E *(Ashfield, Mass.)*

96   SUMMERTIME TREATS

97   HOWES GROCERY (*248 Hampden Street, Holyoke, Mass.*)

98   DANIELS MILL COMPANY (*Hartford, Conn.*)

99   OPEN FOR BUSINESS

100   DECORATION, TOWN HALL (*Ashfield, Mass.*)

101   SHAVE AND A HAIRCUT

102   IN THE PARLOR (*Amherst, Mass.*)

103   AT THE PIANO

104   MARY LYON ROOM, WHITE HOMESTEAD (*Ashfield, Mass.*)

105   LET IN THE LIGHT

106   COZY CORNER (*Southampton, Mass.*)

107   THREE ROOMS

108   THREE CHIMNEYS, EIGHT FLUES

109   CARRIE PRATT'S HOUSE OF PLEASURE (*Holyoke, Mass.*)

110   STARS AND STRIPES

III   GARRETS

112   A VICTORIAN SPLENDOR

113   ''LIGHTNING SPLITTER'' (*Buckland, Mass.*)

114   UNDER THE TREES (*Amherst, Mass.*)

115   ''VISIT NEW YORK STATE''

116   PORTRAIT OF AN ANCESTOR

117   LIGHT IN THE WOODS

118   LAMPPOST AND CHILD IN AUTUMN (*Northfield, Mass.*)

119   TARPAPER HOME

120   THE ROOF SLANTS THREE WAYS

121   SLAVIC WOMAN

122   CROOKED TREE

123   POST-OFFICE TWILIGHT

124   WALTER HOWES AT HIS MOTHER'S HOME (*Gill, Mass.*)

125   SPRINGTIME I (*Williamsburg, Mass.*)

126   SPRINGTIME II (*Northfield, Mass.*)

127   AFTER THE RAIN, YOU CAN SEE FOREVER

128   MILK ... (*Pittsfield, Mass.*)

129   ... AND COOKIES

130   EXPRESS WAGON (*Easthampton, Mass.*)

131   STAGE TIME AT ASHFIELD HOUSE (*Ashfield, Mass.*)

132   MEAT DELIVERY

133   PAINTER (*Easthampton, Mass.*)

134   THE ICE WAGON

135   AT THE ICEHOUSE

136   CLASS PICTURE, CITY SCHOOL

137   RING AROUND THE ROSY

138   PAROCHIAL SCHOOL

139   HOME FOR THE HANDICAPPED

140   ONE-ROOM SCHOOL

141   GRADUATION DAY

142   GIRLS' EXERCISE CLASS

143   BOYS' EXERCISE CLASS

144   FOOTBALL TEAM, SANDERSON ACADEMY (*Ashfield, Mass.*)

145   BASEBALL TEAM, SANDERSON ACADEMY (*Ashfield, Mass.*)

146   CONVENT

147   GENTLEMEN ON THE PORCH OF ASHFIELD HOUSE (*Ashfield, Mass.*)

148   HATS OFF

149   HATS ON

150   THEATER AT THE BRICKYARD

151   VIEWING PLATFORM

152   SECLUDED DINING PAVILION

153   POND SCENE

154   CHICKEN WITH EGG-SHAPED WOODPILE

155   WALTER HOWES ON THE ROLL STONE *(Fitchburg, Mass.)*

156   AMONG THE HYDRANGEAS

157   CONCORD MONUMENT (*Concord, Mass.*)

158   BULLDOG REFLECTING

159   ANOTHER FAMILY PET?

160   CAMPING OUT

161   EYE PATCH, WOMAN, AND CAT

162   A SNAPSHOT

163   I ONLY WANT THE HORSE

164   A COOL SHADED SPOT

165   BOWLER AND STONE WALL (*Williamsburg, Mass.*)

166　TRUMAN BOWMAN (*Ashfield, Mass.*)

168　HARVEST TIME

167　THE RENIFF FAMILY (*Ashfield, Mass.*)

169   A M P U T E E   A N D   F A M I L Y   (*West Springfield, Mass.*)

170   A L L   I N   B L A C K

171   G R A N D M O T H E R I N G   T H E   B A B Y

172   I'LL BE A MILITARY MAN

173   CINDER IN THE EYE

174   TWO TO TAKE CARE OF (*Easthampton, Mass.*)   175   DOWN THE STREET (*West Springfield, Mass.*)

176   THE DIGE CHILDREN (*Ashfield, Mass.*)

177   THE GRAVES BROTHERS
WITH SNOW JUMPERS (*Ashfield, Mass.*)

178   HOWES KIDS MAPLE-SUGARING

179   DOUBLE-RIP SLED AND SNOW JUMPER (*Ashfield, Mass.*)

"PLACES WE HAVE BOARDED AT IN VIEW BUSINESS"

(from Walter K. Howes notebook, 1886–1900)

YEAR	OWNER, ADDRESS	TOWN AND STATE
1886	O. Lillys	Florence, Mass.
	Wm. B. Smith	Orange, Mass.
	John Welch	Northampton, Mass.
1887	Wm. H. Howes	So. Coventry, Ct.
	G. P. Babcock	Vernon, Ct.
	Mrs. Dean	So. Manchester, Ct.
1888	Mrs. Sturtevant	Greenfield, Mass.
	Briggs	Shelburne Falls
	Mrs. Jane Potters	Lennington, Vt.
	Hoosick House (John Turner)	Hoosick Falls, N. Y.
1889	Mrs. Thompson'	Dalton, Mass.
	Mrs. A. L. Houghton	Adams, Mass.
	Mr. A. A. Howes	No. Adams, Mass.
1890	Wm. H. Howes	Northampton, Mass.
		East Hampton
	Mrs. Joe Palmer	So. Hadley Falls
1891	Mrs. Celia Dunham	Springfield, Mass.
	Mrs. Burnett	Springfield, Mass.
	Mr. David Robinson	Thompsonville, Ct.
	Wm. Cantello	Broad Brook, Ct.
	Wm. Levette	Rockville, Ct.
1892	Mrs. J. Roberts	Hartford, Ct.
	Mrs. J. A. Perkens	Middle town, Ct.
	Mr. A. W. Foster	
	R. J. Jones	Meriden, Ct.
1893	Walter Duncan	Indian Orchard, Mass.
	Fred Collises House	Bondville, Mass.
	Jinks House	Warren, Mass.
	Wm. Weld	Brookfield, Mass.
1896	Parady 83 Willow	Woonsocket, R.I.
	Devol 218 Winthrope St.	Taunton, Mass.
1897	110 Prospect St.	Marlboro, Mass.
	Bassett 168 Summer	Fitchburg,
1898	87 Ark St.	Waltham
1899	Metheun St.	Lowell
	708 Belmont St.	Manchester, N.H.
1900	72 Chestnut St.	Florence
	15 Lincoln St.	Greenfield

The photographic achievement of the Howes brothers was made possible, in part, by the timely development and availability of the glass dry-plate negative, a technical innovation that fundamentally changed the nature of photography.

Until 1880 almost all glass photographic negatives were made by a wet-plate (collodion) process. This was a tricky and physically demanding technique: the photographer chemically sensitized a piece of glass in a dark tent or room, then immediately placed the wet plate in a holder. Very quickly the holder was brought out to the camera, which had been set up with its subject composed. After exposure, the photographer rushed the plate back to the darkroom to develop it immediately while the collodion was still wet. Some, like Timothy O'Sullivan and Francis Frith, were able to overcome these difficulties, and when skillfully made, the negatives could yield exquisite results. Photojournalism, though, was of necessity more re-enactment than timely coverage, and most art photography dealt with theatrical allusions to the classics rather than natural or found images.

The wide availability of gelatin dry-plate negatives, based on European advances, revolutionized photography. The plates came precoated with a gelatin emulsion from the plant, and the exposure-development process was vastly simplified and easily learned. The emulsion was more sensitive to light and required much shorter exposure times. An image could be captured at one moment and stored on the plate to be developed at a future time. Interiors could be photographed with strong natural light. Sitters became more comfortable in their environment.

By the early 1880s, factories throughout the East and Midwest in America were mass-producing dry plates. By the end of the decade nearly thirty plants were producing 80 million plates annually.[1] The less expensive process changed the whole economics of photography, which previously had needed subsidies for large survey commissions, and radically altered the range of vision possible. The camera became a democratic tool.

The bounds around the photographer now burst open. Eadweard Muybridge showed the world how people and animals moved. Alfred Stieglitz led a group of photographers beyond the afternoon sun into the rain and snow, to the race track, and through Wall Street traffic. Eugène Atget captured the morning light of Paris.

Commercial photography burgeoned outside the studio. For a modest investment, perhaps no more than $100, one could start an "artistic photography" business, and when orders declined in the studio, take to the road soliciting commissions or selling existing "views" (postcards). No previous experience or training was needed, as John Szarkowski has pointed out: "Those who invented photography were scientists and painters, but its professional practitioners were a different lot . . . converted silversmiths, tinkers, druggists, blacksmiths and printers. If photography was a new artistic problem, such men had the advantage of having nothing to unlearn."[2]

Alvah Howes left his frugal farm labors for the greener pastures of photography in the 1880s. He began as a studio photographer specializing in babies, but quickly diversified to cabinet photographs of the whole family, to crayon

[1] William Welling, *Photography in America: The Formative Years, 1839–1900* (New York: Thomas Y. Crowell Co., 1978), p. 294.

[2] John Szarkowski, introduction to *The Photographer's Eye* (New York: Museum of Modern Art, 1966).

(hand-tinted) portraits, and to views of shops, local topography, and the area mills. He always advertised as an "artistic photographer," which suggested to his customers inventive studio props, backgrounds, and lighting. He used a wide variety of camera formats from miniature to 16 by 20 inches.

We know little of Alvah's professional training or stylistic antecedents other than a possible apprenticeship with Elliott W. Cook (see Introduction) or G. L. Chapman, whose Turners Falls studio he first acquired. It is hard to imagine that he had missed seeing the photographic documentation of the Mill River flood of 1874 by A. E. Alden of Springfield, Massachusetts.[3] The flood wiped out many of the mills and factories in the region just south of Ashfield, and Alden's coverage of the event is considered a landmark in commercial news photography. His stereographs of the tragedy suggest the Howes way of seeing in their creation of a strong balance between person, architecture, and landscape. This formal device makes many of the photographs neither portraits nor architectural pictures, but instead establishes dynamic relationships between home and dweller, worker and tool, farmer and land.

The photographs are of a remarkable and consistently high technical standard, with careful attention to detail, clarity of presentation, a feeling for the subtlety of light and tonal variances of the subjects. They share some of the documentary concerns of Eugène Atget, yet the handling of groups seems more closely related to the precise choreography of Frances Benjamin Johnson, a pioneer photojournalist. Whereas Atget had to make peace with himself as an artist with a mission, often returning to photograph the same tree or street over and over again, the Howeses had to satisfy clients and work quickly.

A well-to-do family pose with their servants and their white horse (no. 8). The picture is a careful construct of social hierarchy, profound gestures, and figures assembled adroitly in a recreational space. It is full of facts and relationships. The man of the house (or chief servant?) is placed squarely in the center. The woman who stands is framed gracefully by a dark space. The photographer must have known light, perspective—and protocol. We can guess at the occupations, and a costume historian could probably fix the date by the dress. And, as so often in American history, a black person is in the rear.

The dog trainer (no. 40) makes a very different, almost modern composition. Here the photographer had presumably less cooperative sitters, yet the ropes, dogs, and posts describe a rhythmically hypnotic space. The man's face is simultaneously with us and turned to the dog he holds, reflecting the last heroic attempt before the camera to cheat time and show the hounds. The photograph reaches us at many levels of appreciation: as a geometric dance; as information on tying dogs and on varieties of hounds; and as a drama of the moment, a uniquely photographic concern.

Darius Kinsey, the great photographer of the American Northwest logging camps, exclaimed, "You aren't a logger until you own a dollar watch and have your picture taken with a tree."[4] The Howes photographs share the same mating of laborers and tools, and a reverence for work, implements, and environment. In one picture (no. 59), loggers gather about a fallen tree and one about to be cut down. A lumberman flashes back the sun to the camera with his polished axehead: it is the quintessence of pride in one's tools. The photograph also says the way to fell a tree is with two cuts, one on each side of the trunk, the second cut slightly higher than the first and on the side of the intended descent. How can you know this? Look at the stump in the lower left corner.

The elements and composition of group portraits in many Howes photographs raise as many questions as they answer. What significance is attached, for example, to the embroidered college pillows in no. 9? Whose portrait

---

[3] Welling, *Photography in America*, p. 231.

[4] Ralph Andrews, *Photographers in the Frontier West* (Seattle, Wash.: Superior Publishing Co., 1965).

is being displayed by the woman in no. 116? What about the relationship between people and houses, where we sometimes glimpse walks and yards, sometimes just a porch, sometimes see both house and owner dwarfed by a huge tree or bush?

The Howes brothers had a talent for the cooperative portrait and the nonpretentious direction of their subjects. On first inspection the poses seem stilted and expression-less to us. We have been weaned on the snapshot with all its implied verities—isn't Daddy's picture of Mommy and me "the way things really were" that day? Or is it the way we would prefer to remember them? When we spend time with the Howeses' work, we find in it a surprising range of expression, spontaneity, and unforced emotion—qualities which reflect "the way things were" with true authority.

ALAN B. NEWMAN

An obvious strength of the Howes collection is its magnitude. The more than 21,000 negatives now owned by the Ashfield Historical Society make it by far the largest turn-of-the-century dry-plate archive by a single photographer or photographic concern in America. The quality of the images is of a consistently high standard.

Regrettably, few of the millions of glass negatives made by early photographers have survived intact. Scavengers often destroyed the image by scraping the emulsion from the negative plate, since both the glass and the silver had more apparent value in their elemental forms. The new enemy of photographic preservation is simply improper storage in a hostile atmospheric environment. Humidity breaks down the stability of gelatin emulsions and provides a nurturing climate for micro-organisms. Instead of food for thought, negatives and photographs become sustenance for spores and molds.

By great good fortune the larger portion of the Howes work survived the years intact, stored in the dry attic of the Zachariah Field Tavern in Ashfield, the last studio-residence of Alvah Howes. In the early 1960s, the collection was donated and transferred to the newly purchased Ashfield Historical Society Museum.

During the last sixteen years, a concerted effort has been made to identify the sites in the negatives. Theodore Hendrick of the Southampton (Massachusetts) Historical Society has performed much of this task, using clues in the negatives themselves. The Howeses used the edges of the plate to record information: each carried a negative number and occasionally a year. Another number, probably referring to the number of prints a client had ordered, appears often on the opposite edge. In the absence of company records, Hendrick guessed that adjacent plate numbers (their system was chronological) could mean geographical proximity as well. Selecting readily known sites such as churches and monuments (he was inspired early on when he discovered his own house pictured), he traveled to those places with proofs of neighboring numbers in hand. Working in this way as a photoarchaeologist, he has been able to identify nearly a third of the collection.

Initially, as sites were identified, those plates were given to the historical society in that particular town; 5,000 negatives were dispersed in this way. In 1977, the Ashfield Historical Society began mobilizing efforts to reunite the collection and restore its unique value as a research tool. They also began to raise interest in preserving their own holdings: at that point more than 17,000 glass negatives and 300 vintage prints, then stored improperly in wooden apple crates.

A massive grassroots volunteer effort succeeded in matching grants from the National Historical Publications and Records Commission and the Massachusetts Council on the Arts and Humanities. Hundreds of private individuals and small businesses gave in support of the Howes Brothers Photographic Preservation Project. The goals were to clean and preserve the negatives, build a storage environment with controlled temperature and humidity, film all the images onto a fine-grained motion-picture stock that could be viewed on standard microfilm readers, produce a study set of prints, catalogue all the information in the photographs, and create, with the aid of computers, a descriptive and retrieval system that would facilitate the countless research possibilities.

The Ashfield Historical Society has now met or is close to realizing each of these goals. The use of high-quality motion-picture stock to copy directly from the negatives is a pioneering photographic study tool. It allows the research community easy access to the information in the photographs without jeopardizing the safety of the original material. Extremely cost-efficient, it produces copies of surprisingly good quality.

The entire Howes collection can be viewed on microfilm at the University of Massachusetts library in Amherst and the Greenfield (Massachusetts) Community College library. A synopsis of the collection, which includes 650 images selected to convey a variety of subject matter and geography, along with retrieval aids and Howes biographical material, is available for purchase as one 100-foot microform roll.

A NOTE ON PLATINUM TONING

The Howes brothers used a photographic paper, Aristotype, which was of the "printing-out" variety, com-

monly known today as a P.O.P. paper. It had a collodion chloride silver emulsion, and the printing technician would make use of the sun for exposure. Aristotype made possible extraordinary delicacy in the rendering of both shadows and highlights. The color was close to that of a cantaloupe's meat, but it could be enhanced toward purple or neutral brown with a toning bath of salts of gold or platinum.

Kodak's Studio Proof is the only P.O.P. paper commercially available today. The gold toning of Studio Proof has enjoyed a considerable renaissance in popularity over the last twenty years, as has the hand sensitizing of artists' papers to produce platinum prints. It is only inevitable that today's platinum printers who wish to turn to "noble metal toning" of P.O.P. should revive the platinum toning techniques of the early century.

HOWES BROTHERS PHOTOGRAPHS ORDERING INFORMATION

Prices are guaranteed through June 30, 1981, subject to change if there are major fluctuations in the precious-metals market. When ordering, please refer to the negative number given in the list following this price information.

Photographic prints made directly from Howes negatives

Contact reproduction-quality archival silver
    print (4¼″ x 6½″ image on 8 x 10 paper) $25.00

Contact museum-quality archival platinum or

platinum-toned P.O.P. print in 2-ply museum
    board overmat (4¼″ x 6½″ image)   100.00

Museum-quality enlarged platinum or P.O.P.
    print (10″ x 12″ image) in 2-ply museum
    board overmat   175.00

Inexpensive research prints

Enlargement 4¼″ x 6½″ image on 8 x 10 paper from
    copy 35mm negative for study purposes only   6.00

Enlargement 8″ x 12″ image on 11 x 14 paper
made from copy 35mm negative for study
purposes only   12.00

Microform duplicates from the collection

One 100′ *Synopsis* of the collection on 35mm
motion picture stock suitable for use in
standard microfilm readers (approximately
700 images)   150.00

Catalogue for *Synopsis* roll   15.00

The entire negative collection owned by the
Ashfield Historical Society, 29 100′ microform
rolls. Includes catalogue, finding aids   (Write)

For order blank and a brochure concerning the Howes
photographs write: Howes Project, Ashfield, MA 01330.

The following list gives the original numbers which the
Howes brothers used themselves on their negatives and
which have been retained in cataloguing the collection.
Suffix letters have been added arbitrarily to distinguish between duplicate numbers. Please refer to the Howes negative number when ordering prints from the collection.

CAPTION / NEGATIVE		CAPTION / NEGATIVE	
1	4152B	13	2573C
2	6556C	14	3603B
3	4085A	15	312C
4	6955	16	6682C
5	858C	17	3343B
6	4260B	18	6660
7	5366A	19	1812E
8	3129C	20	4051B
9	2773B	21	3928B
10	1923C	22	1364E
11	4811	23	2221C
12	2776C	24	3313B

CAPTION / NEGATIVE		CAPTION / NEGATIVE	
25	161C	63	V700
26	2134A	64	3141B
27	5F	65	3142B
28	5248C	66	884C
29	2828F	67	3480A
30	2759A	68	1806A
31	486D	68A	6005A
32	9001	69	V2336
33	361F	70	1806C
34	6235A	71	355A
35	4185C	72	4384A
36	6519A	73	5595A
37	4199A	74	5391B
38	2500A	75	5392B
39	1456B	76	5393
40	1150E	77	298B
41	3070C	78	5201B
42	3302A	79	6123C
43	952A	80	4744
44	3221B	81	102E
45	1030C	82	417X
46	1752C	83	1230A
47	5071B	84	5218B
48	5073B	85	W35-1
49	5059B	86	1029P
50	V3819	87	5248B
51	229H	88	199B
52	855D	89	5678C
53	4135C	90	VP58
54	1526B	91	5007A
55	W5086	92	5383A
56	874P	93	9002
57	5495B	94	4158B
58	4816A	95	3F
59	58E	96	2629D
60	1361A	97	3044B
61	2467D	98	2321B
62	2513C	99	1038C

ORDERING INFORMATION

CAPTION	NEGATIVE		CAPTION	NEGATIVE		CAPTION	NEGATIVE		CAPTION	NEGATIVE
100	9022		120	1934A		140	93F		160	4048A
101	800C		121	1159D		141	3930A		161	1558C
102	2841D		122	2656B		142	1766D		162	927D
103	3596B		123	6080A		143	V1763		163	2047D
104	V71		124	4719		144	74D		164	5356B
105	4179B		125	455B		145	V93		165	68A
106	1167E		126	5138B		146	4047B		166	16G
107	1602A		127	2583B		147	9014		167	5989A
108	6467		128	1411A		148	7038		168	4862A
109	3123B		129	5384C		149	7039		169	3141C
110	1542C		130	2514P		150	2075A		170	5029B
111	4157A		131	W12-1		151	4243C		171	50F
112	2633D		132	1431E		152	2990B		172	1113B
113	2058A		133	809Q		153	1668B		173	5378B
114	3038D		134	3558C		154	W40-4		174	431P
115	17B		135	2553A		155	W36-1		175	5669B
116	5232B		136	1880B		156	W31-5		176	9527
117	5845B		137	1351D		157	W947		177	9545
118	5132B		138	1438B		158	118E		178	W34-1
119	62G		139	2030B		159	686C		179	9006

ABOUT THE CONTRIBUTORS

Alan B. Newman is director of the Howes Brothers Photographic Preservation Project. In addition to overseeing the preservation, cataloguing, and microfilming of the 21,000 glass negatives in the Howes collection, he printed the 200 images reproduced in this volume. He is also on the photography faculty of the New School for Social Research and of Pratt Institute, in New York. He has been the recipient of a photography fellowship from the National Endowment for the Arts. His special interest is platinum printing, and his photographs have been exhibited in galleries throughout the Northeast. He lives in Ashfield, Massachusetts.

Gerald McFarland is a professor of history at the University of Massachusetts, Amherst, and a former chairman of the history department there. He is the author of *Mugwumps, Morals, and Politics, 1884–1920* (University of Massachusetts Press) and editor of *Moralists or Pragmatists? The Mugwumps, 1884–1900* (Simon & Schuster). He lives in Leverett, Massachusetts.

Richard Wilbur is one of America's most distinguished poets, authors, and critics. He has received, in addition to numerous international honors, the Pulitzer Prize, the National Book Award, and the Bollingen Prize in Poetry. A member of the National Institute of Arts and Letters and former president of the American Academy of Arts and Letters, he lives in Cummington, Massachusetts.